VERSUS!

T0005303

Jellyfish vs. Cobra

Marla Coppolino

**BLACK
RABBIT
BOOKS**

Hi Jinx is published by Black Rabbit Books
P.O. Box 227, Mankato, Minnesota, 56002.
www.blackrabbitbooks.com
Copyright © 2022 Black Rabbit Books

Gina Kammer and Marysa Storm, editors;
Michael Sellner, designer and photo researcher

All rights reserved. No part of this book may be reproduced in any
form without written permission from the publisher.

Library of Congress Cataloging-in-Publication Data
Names: Coppolino, Marla, author.
Title: Jellyfish vs. cobra / by Marla Coppolino.
Other titles: Jellyfish versus cobra
Description: Mankato, Minnesota : Black Rabbit Books, [2022] |
Series: Hi jinx. versus! | Includes bibliographical references and
index. | Audience: Ages 8-12 | Audience: Grades 4-6 |
Summary: "Struggling or reluctant readers will laugh and
learn as they explore the features and adaptations of the
slippery jellyfish and the slithering cobra through playful
illustrations, engaging text, and a unique spin on animal
information"— Provided by publisher.
Identifiers: LCCN 2020017461 (print) | LCCN 2020017462
(ebook) | ISBN 9781623107307 (library binding) |
ISBN 9781644665732 (paperback) | ISBN 9781623107369
(ebook) Subjects: LCSH: Jellyfishes—Juvenile literature. |
Cobras—Juvenile literature.
Classification: LCC QL377.S4 C75 2022 (print) |
LCC QL377.S4 (ebook) | DDC 593.5/3—dc23
LC record available at https://lccn.loc.gov/2020017461
LC ebook record available at
https://lccn.loc.gov/2020017462

Image Credits

Alamy: Dinodia Photos, 2–3; Portis Imaging, 3; Roberto
Fumagalli, 16–17; Stocktrek Images, Inc., 7; WaterFrame,
11; Dreamstime: Ansie Martin, 17; Tigatelu, Cover, 19;
Minden Pictures: Daniel Heuclin, 11; Nature Picture Library:
Guy Edwardes, 11; Shutterstock: Angeliki Vel, 12–13; Arcady,
13; CappaPhoto, 15; CarryLove, 15; Christos Georghiou, 4,
23; designer_an, 7; ekler, 10; Eric Isselee, 9; frescomovie, Cover;
Kateryna Kon, 1; Kieran Jack, 8; mejnak, 12; Memo Angeles, 7, 8, 9,
11, 20; mrjo, 1, 4, 6, 12–13, 14, 23; Nadya Dobrynina, 21; Natykach
Nataliia, 5; Nearbirds, 4–5; owatta, 18–19; Pasko Maksim, 23, 24;
picoStudio, 9; Pitju, 21; REYYARTS, 21; Ron Dale, 5, 6, 18, 20; Teguh
Mujiono, 21; totallypic, 6, 15, 17, 18, 19; Tueris, 14; White Space
Illustrations, Cover, 18; twitter.com: Easternguy, 20

Contents

Chapter 1
The Swish or the Slither

Jellyfish sting. Cobras bite. These are very different animals. But they are both incredibly dangerous. You wouldn't want to be surprised by either one. Imagine if we put these two animals in the ring. Which one would win the fight?

Chapter 2
Comparing Their Features

Let's start by comparing their sizes. Jellyfish come in all kinds of sizes. Some are really tiny. But others are huge. The lion's mane jelly can be up to 120 feet (37 meters) long. That's longer than two school buses!

Cobras are big snakes. The king cobra is the longest **venomous** snake in the world. It grows up to 18 feet (5 m) long.

120 feet

A jellyfish's body is about 95 percent water.

Dangerous Features

Both of these animals have scary features. Cobras can practically stand up. They lift one third of their bodies off the ground. And they can slither forward like that! Their sharp fangs don't make them look friendly either.

Jellies have wavy tentacles. Those arms might not seem scary. But those tentacles carry sharp darts.

Deadly Poisons

Cobras and jellies both have deadly venom. Jellies' tentacle darts are full of poison. The animals use the poison to **stun** or kill **prey**. It can kill people who get in the way too.

Cobras also use venom to kill. Most cobras bite and **inject** the poison. But some of these snakes spit. They shoot venom into attackers' eyes.

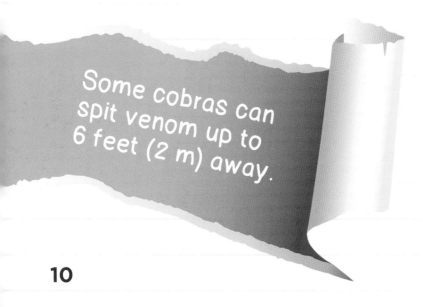

Some cobras can spit venom up to 6 feet (2 m) away.

jellyfish killing prey

cobra bite

cobra spitting

Fast and Furious

Don't take your eyes off an attacking cobra. It's not the fastest snake in the world. But it's still very quick. It can strike from a standing position in just seconds.

Jellyfish might have the fastest attack in the world, though. Their darts fire the moment they touch prey. These darts travel faster than bullets.

A jelly's darts can still fire after it has died.

Good Senses

Jellies don't actually have brains.

But they do have tools to notice things around them. Areas on the edges of their bells can **detect** light. They can also sense **hormones**.

Cobras have great eyesight and a strong **sense** of smell. For example, the king cobra can see prey that's more than 300 feet (91 m) away. The snake's long, forked tongue picks up smells in the air.

jellyfish bell

At Home

Cobras only live in southern Africa and southeast Asia. Many make their homes in rain forests. But they all like to be near water.

Jellyfish live in all the world's oceans. There are thousands of different kinds of jellies. They drift along **currents**. Since they don't have brains, they don't really decide where to live.

Chapter 3

Who Would Win?

Jellyfish and cobras both have incredible features. Who would win?

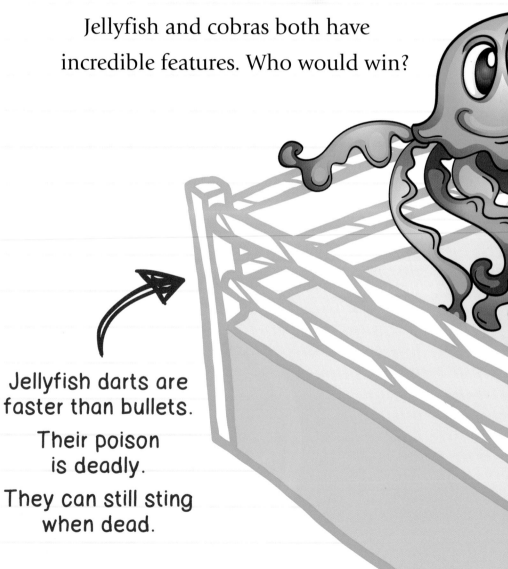

Jellyfish darts are faster than bullets.

Their poison is deadly.

They can still sting when dead.

Cobras have great eyesight and sense of smell.

Some can spray their deadly venom.

They are quick and long.

Chapter 4
Get in on the Hi Jinx

Venom is dangerous, but scientists study ways to use it. Jellyfish venom has ingredients that can fight **cancer**. And parts of both jellyfish and cobra venom can relieve pain. Lots of research still needs to be done. But you might thank a jellyfish or a cobra someday. Their venom might help pain go away.

Take It One Step More

1. Jellies and cobras can be dangerous to humans. Do you think humans should try to get rid of them? Why or why not?

2. Why do you think jellyfish have such a large range?

3. What do jellyfish and cobras have in common?

GLOSSARY

cancer (KAN-sur)—a serious, and sometimes deadly, disease

current (KUR-uhnt)—the part of a fluid body, such as air or water, moving continuously in a certain direction

detect (dee-TEKT)—to discover the existence or presence of something

hormone (HOR-mohn)—a chemical substance produced by body cells and released especially into the blood and having a specific effect on cells or organs of the body

inject (IN-jekt)—to force a liquid into something

prey (PRAY)—an animal hunted or killed for food

sense (SENS)—one of five natural powers from which a person or animal receives information; the five senses are touch, taste, smell, sight, and hearing.

stun (STUHN)—to make senseless or dizzy

venomous (VEN-uh-mus)—containing venom or poison

BOOKS

Downs, Kieran. *King Cobra vs. Mongoose.* Animal Battles. Minneapolis: Bellwether Media, 2022.

Gail, Terp. *Cobras.* Slithering Snakes. Mankato, MN: Black Rabbit Books, 2021.

Zobel, Derek. *Jellyfish.* Ocean Animals. Minneapolis: Bellwether Media, Inc., 2021.

WEBSITES

Cobra
animals.sandiegozoo.org/animals/cobra

Jellies
www.montereybayaquarium.org/animals/animals-a-to-z/jellies

King Cobra
kids.nationalgeographic.com/animals/reptiles/king-cobra/

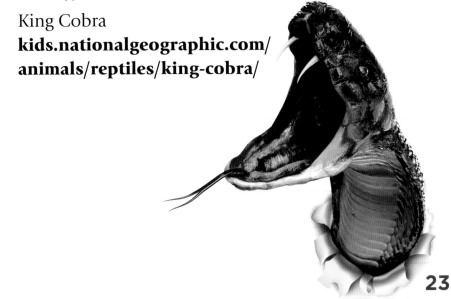